CCSS **Genre** Expository

Essential Question
Why are rules important?

MW00682333

Government RULES

by Anton Wilson

Chapter 1
Rules Protect Us

The government makes rules to keep people safe.

Rules help people get along. They make life safer. When everyone follows rules, people know what to expect. They have the same goals. This can make life better.

Our country's government formed rules that you and your family follow every day. Some rules protect public places. Some rules help keep foods and medicines safe. Some rules protect people's ideas or inventions. Some help protect our environment. These rules help protect animals in their natural habitats.

People visit Yellowstone National Park to see the geyser known as "Old Faithful."

National Parks

Have you ever visited a national park? Rules protect these parks. They are built on land that is open to the public. The world's first national park was Yellowstone National Park. It was founded in the United States in 1872.

Every state except Delaware has at least one national park. The state with the most national parks is California. Washington, D.C., has four national parks. America's largest national park is in Alaska. It stretches over more than 13 million acres of land!

Top 5 Most Visited National Parks (2010)

- Great Smoky Mountains

- Grand Canyon

- Yosemite

- Yellowstone

- Rocky Mountains

When people think of parks, they may picture green trees, mountains, or even deserts. But some national parks don't look like this. They are built around monuments, battlefields, or other sites from history. Even roads can be national parks. That's why some roads are called parkways.

Today, the United States has almost 400 national parks. Some are places of natural beauty, such as the Grand Canyon. Others, such as the Statue of Liberty, are part of our country's history. The National Park Service has rules to protect these important places. That way people can enjoy them in the future.

Chapter 2
Food and Medicine Rules

The USDA stamp lets you know the meat was checked.

Did you know that there are rules to make sure that your food is safe to eat? The United States Department of Agriculture (USDA) checks meat, poultry (such as chicken), and eggs. You can see the USDA stamp on some items sold at the supermarket.

What does this stamp mean? It tells you the meat is safe to eat and free of disease. The stamp promises people that the label on the package is correct.

William Thomas Cain/Getty Images News/Getty Images

It is important to eat a good breakfast and lunch to help you learn.

School Lunches

The USDA also makes rules that schools must follow. Public schools often provide meals to students. Schools that follow USDA rules get extra food and money. This allows them to offer free or low-cost breakfasts and lunches to students.

Food Safety

The USDA informs people how to handle and prepare foods safely. It produces fact sheets on food safety.

For example, some foods can be dangerous if they are eaten raw. Foods such as eggs, pork, or chicken must be cooked to a certain temperature. After handling raw meat or eggs, people should wash their hands. They should wash cutting boards and kitchen counters. These steps kill germs. Following food safety rules can save lives!

It is important to follow food safety rules when handling raw meat.

How to Store Eggs Safely

Type of Egg	Can be refrigerated for	Can be frozen for
raw egg	3–5 weeks (in shell)	1 year (out of shell)
hard-boiled egg	1 week	do not freeze
store-bought eggnog	3–5 days	6 months

The government gives us information about how to store and serve food safely. Did you ever wonder how long certain foods can be kept in the refrigerator? The government provides these facts, as in the chart above. You can find out what temperature meats such as beef and chicken must reach before they can be safely eaten.

Medicines

Some medicines help people get better when they are sick. A doctor says what kind of medicine to take, and people buy the medicine at a drugstore. So who makes sure medicines are safe? The government has rules about medicine safety.

The Food and Drug Administration (FDA) tests medicines, or drugs. Drugs cannot be sold or prescribed until the FDA says so. The FDA checks for possible **side effects** and figures out how much of a medicine people should take. Finally, after testing, the FDA may **approve** a drug. Then it can be used.

The FDA creates guides to help people understand the rules for taking medicines.

Chapter 3
Animal Rules

You need to get special permission to fish at some lakes.

You live in the United States. But it isn't just your home. It's also home to animals and plants. The U.S. Fish and Wildlife Service protects natural habitats.

U.S. Fish and Wildlife is a government agency. Its purpose is to protect nature in America. This agency creates rules about hunting and fishing. People must get a written **permit** for these activities. If they are caught without a permit, they will have to pay a fine.

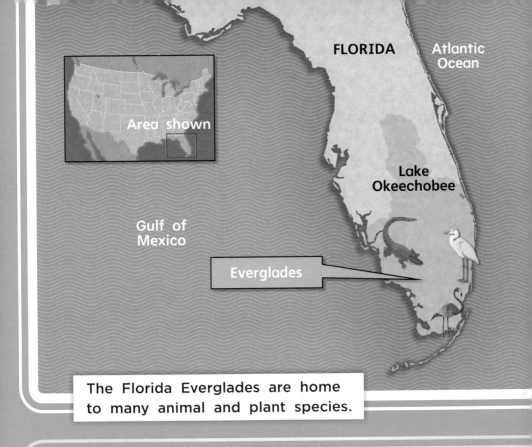

The Florida Everglades are home to many animal and plant species.

The U.S. Fish and Wildlife Service also protects birds and their wetland habitats. Some swamps are protected. People who want to canoe or camp there need a special permit. They must obey rules. That way, they do not harm living things in this special place.

The U.S. government also keeps lists of endangered plants and animals. These are species that may die out soon. Right now there are more than 1,000 of these species. Government rules help to protect them.

Chapter 4
Idea Rules

A book's copyright page usually comes right after the title page.

Did you know that government rules also protect ideas? Artists use ideas in paintings, and musicians turn ideas into songs. Writers use ideas in books. Copyright rules protect these people's ideas.

Think of a book you love. If you look inside, you'll see a **copyright** page. When the author first exclaimed, "I have an idea!" he or she probably wasn't thinking about copyright. But copyright rules protect writers. They make it illegal for someone else to copy and sell the book without permission.

Andersen Ross/Photodisc/Getty Images

Companies trademark their brand names so no one else can use the names.

Other rules protect inventions. The U.S. Patent and Trademark Office will give an inventor a patent, which is a paper that says the inventor owns his or her invention. A patent protects an idea.

If you invented a new product, would you want other people to copy your idea? Of course not! It is your invention, so you should be able to make money from it. That's also true for books, artworks, and business ideas.

How Ideas Are Protected

Copyright: Protects an author's written work

Patent: Protects an inventor's invention

Trademark: Protects a business's name, logo, slogan

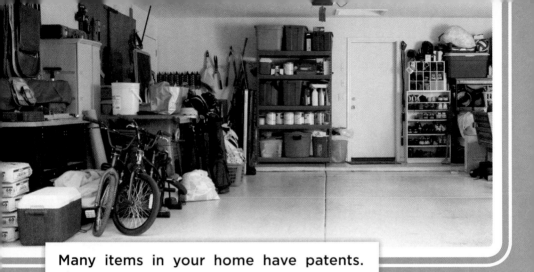

Many items in your home have patents.

How does a patent protect ideas? It prevents someone from making money from another person's invention. No one else can make, use, or sell it without the inventor's permission.

Our government issues three types of patents. Utility patents are for new, useful things and ideas. Design patents are for new designs or decorations. Plant patents are for new kinds of plants. For example, farmers may grow new types of fruits and vegetables.

Whether rules protect ideas or people, they help improve our lives. Government rules protect our health and safety and our rights. By following rules, you help make our world a better place.

Summarize

Use important details to summarize *Government Rules*.

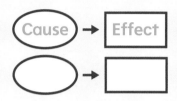

Text Evidence

1. How do you know *Government Rules* is expository text? GENRE

2. What caused the government to create rules about food? CAUSE AND EFFECT

3. Use what you know of multiple-meaning words to figure out the meaning of *fine* on page 10. MULTIPLE-MEANING WORDS

4. Why is it important to have rules that protect national parks? WRITE ABOUT READING

Compare Texts
Read about why rules at the pool are important.

POOL RULES

Going swimming at a pool is a fun way to cool off on a hot day. But if you swim, you must follow rules. That way, everyone stays safe and has fun.

Pool rules are usually posted on a sign that everyone can see. Some pool signs use symbols. These catch people's attention.

Many cities have public pools.

Diving

Some pools have a deep end with a diving board. In other pools, the water is not deep enough for diving. People who dive in shallow water can get badly hurt. The "No Diving" rule helps keep people safe.

Running

The safe way to get around a pool is to walk slowly. Running near a pool is dangerous. A person could slip on the wet deck and fall. People can break an arm or leg this way. That's why the "No Running" sign is important.

Eating and Drinking

Most pools do not allow people to eat or drink in the pool area. Dropping food or drinks in the pool makes the water dirty.

Eating or drinking on the pool deck is a bad idea. People can slip on spilled food, and glass bottles might break. Bare feet and broken glass are a bad combination! Most pools have special areas where you can get a snack or a drink.

Make Connections

Why are pool rules important? ESSENTIAL QUESTION

How are the rules in *Government Rules* similar to the rules in *Pool Rules*? TEXT TO TEXT

Glossary

approve *(uh-PROOV)* to accept something or judge it to be good *(page 9)*

copyright *(KOP-ee-right)* owning something that you have written so that you can make money from it *(page 12)*

permit *(PUR-mit)* a written note that allows someone to do something *(page 10)*

side effects *(SIGHD uh-fekts)* extra effects of a medicine on the body, usually harmful *(page 9)*

Index

Focus on
Social Studies

Purpose To find out why classroom rules are important

What to Do

Step 1 List at least three classroom rules.

Step 2 Write the rules in the first column of a chart like this one.

Rule	How It Helps

Step 3 In the second column, write one way each rule helps you and your class.

Step 4 Discuss what you learned with a classmate.